# Dwell

## Bible Study & Prayer

# JOURNAL

A Guided Journal for Study,
Scripture meditation & Prayer

## Jenny Erlingsson

# Dwell: Bible Study & Prayer Journal

This book is available at: www.milkandhoneybooks.com and other online retailers
Cover & Interior Designed by Jenny Erlingsson via Canva

Reach us on the Internet: www.milkandhoneybooks.com
ISBN 13: 978-1-7346780-8-6

For Worldwide Distribution, Printed in the United States of America
1 2 3 4 5 6 7 8 9 10

# Dwell
## Bible Study & Prayer
## JOURNAL

THIS BEAUTY BELONGS TO:

# Hey Friend!

I'M SO THANKFUL THAT YOU ARE POSITIONING YOURSELF TO GO DEEPER IN YOUR STUDY OF THE BIBLE. IT IS AMAZING HOW MUCH WE CAN GAIN FROM FOCUSED AND INTENTIONAL TIME DWELLING WITH GOD. HIS WORD IS WHAT WE NEED TO WALK OUT OUR LIVES WITH HOPE, PEACE AND CONFIDENCE, HOPEFULLY CHANGING ATMOSPHERES WITH GOD'S PRESENCE AS WE GO.

EACH PAGE OF THIS JOURNAL GIVES YOU OPPORTUNITY TO **WRITE** DOWN VERSES OR PASSAGES THAT YOU WANT TO STUDY FURTHER. THE **PONDER & PRAY** QUESTIONS INVITE YOU TO DEEPLY ENGAGE IN WHAT IS BEING REVEALED TO YOU BY THE HOLY SPIRIT. THERE IS SPACE AT THE END OF EACH WEEK TO **JOURNAL** (OR DOODLE OR DRAW) AS YOU FEEL LED TO.

IN THE BACK OF THIS JOURNAL YOU WILL FIND THE "TREE OF ABIDING" CREATIVE EXERCISE TO DOCUMENT FAVORITE VERSES. THERE IS NO SET WAY TO DO THIS. THE FOCUS IS **JESUS** AND THE GOAL IS CULTIVATION, MOVING THINGS AROUND AND OUT OF YOUR LIFE AS YOU GROW IN YOUR RELATIONSHIP WITH HIM.

♡Jenny

I'm that girl.
tapping your shoulder from behind,
whispering in your ear "You can do this."
I'm that girl.
who believes the little things matter and our
frustrated places can become sacred spaces where
we sacrifice our will for His..
I'm that girl.
who always believes there is more. Who refuses to
take moments at face value but searches for the
eternal value in each happening.
Let's be those girls.
Ashy, calloused praying knees, who help their
sisters in this fight to keep on shining.
Shining bright, building up an inferno in the night.

"Whoever **Dwells** in the shelter of the Most High will rest in the shadow of the Almighty. I will say of the Lord, "He is my refuge and my fortress, my God, in **whom I trust**"

Psalm 91:1&2 Niv

# Dwell

"I HAVE HIDDEN YOUR WORD IN MY HEART THAT I MIGHT NOT SIN AGAINST YOU."

*Psalm 119:11 Niv*

6

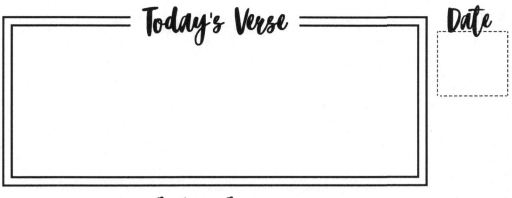

## Today's Verse

### Date

## Ponder & Pray

START WITH WORSHIP. TELL THE LORD HOW YOU FEEL ABOUT HIM.
THANK HIM FOR WHAT THIS VERSE SHOWS YOU ABOUT HIS NATURE.

_____
_____
_____
_____

LORD, WHAT DO YOU HAVE TO SAY TO ME THROUGH THIS VERSE?

_____
_____
_____
_____

WHAT ARE SOME WAYS I CAN PLANT THIS TRUTH DEEP IN MY HEART?

_____
_____
_____
_____

WHAT IS GOING ON IN MY LIFE THAT I NEED TO APPLY THIS VERSE TO?

_____
_____
_____
_____

**Date**

## Today's Verse

### Ponder & Pray

Start with Worship. Tell the Lord how you feel about Him.
Thank Him for what this verse shows you about His nature.

_____

_____

_____

_____

Lord, what do you have to say to me through this verse?

_____

_____

_____

_____

What are some ways I can plant this truth deep in my heart?

_____

_____

_____

_____

What is going on in my life that I need to apply this verse to?

_____

_____

_____

_____

# Today's Verse

**Date**

## Ponder & Pray

START WITH WORSHIP. TELL THE LORD HOW YOU FEEL ABOUT HIM. THANK HIM FOR WHAT THIS VERSE SHOWS YOU ABOUT HIS NATURE.

LORD, WHAT DO YOU HAVE TO SAY TO ME THROUGH THIS VERSE?

WHAT ARE SOME WAYS I CAN PLANT THIS TRUTH DEEP IN MY HEART?

WHAT IS GOING ON IN MY LIFE THAT I NEED TO APPLY THIS VERSE TO?

**Date**

## Today's Verse

## Ponder & Pray

Start with Worship. Tell the Lord how you feel about Him.
Thank Him for what this verse shows you about His nature.

_____

_____

_____

_____

Lord, what do you have to say to me through this verse?

_____

_____

_____

_____

What are some ways I can plant this truth deep in my heart?

_____

_____

_____

_____

_____

What is going on in my life that I need to apply this verse to?

_____

_____

_____

_____

_____

## Today's Verse

**Date**

### Ponder & Pray

Start with Worship. Tell the Lord how you feel about Him.
Thank Him for what this verse shows you about His nature.

_____
_____
_____
_____

Lord, what do you have to say to me through this verse?

_____
_____
_____
_____

What are some ways I can plant this truth deep in my heart?

_____
_____
_____
_____

What is going on in my life that I need to apply this verse to?

_____
_____
_____
_____

**Date**

## Today's Verse

### Ponder & Pray

Start with Worship. Tell the Lord how you feel about Him. Thank Him for what this verse shows you about His nature.

_____
_____
_____
_____

Lord, what do you have to say to me through this verse?

_____
_____
_____
_____

What are some ways I can plant this truth deep in my heart?

_____
_____
_____
_____

What is going on in my life that I need to apply this verse to?

_____
_____
_____
_____

# Journal

Take time to sit, rest, breathe...be before the Lord.
What does he have to say to you?

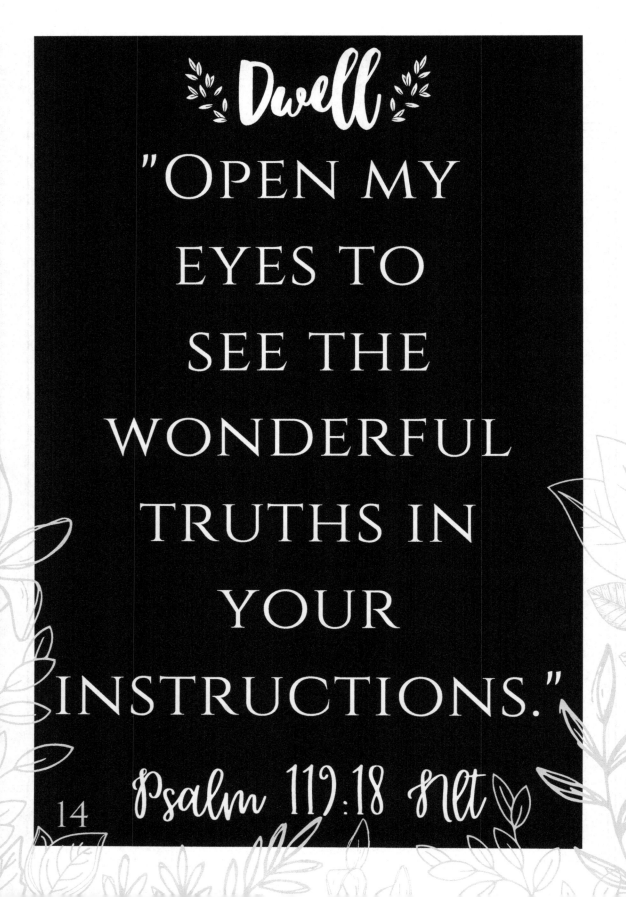

*Dwell*

"OPEN MY EYES TO SEE THE WONDERFUL TRUTHS IN YOUR INSTRUCTIONS."

Psalm 119:18 NLt

14

## Today's Verse

### Date

## Ponder & Pray

Start with Worship. Tell the Lord how you feel about Him.
Thank Him for what this verse shows you about His nature.

_____
_____
_____
_____

Lord, what do you have to say to me through this verse?

_____
_____
_____
_____

What are some ways I can plant this truth deep in my heart?

_____
_____
_____
_____
_____

What is going on in my life that I need to apply this verse to?

_____
_____
_____
_____

**Date**

## Today's Verse

### Ponder & Pray

Start with Worship. Tell the Lord how you feel about Him.
Thank Him for what this verse shows you about His nature.

_____
_____
_____
_____

Lord, what do you have to say to me through this verse?

_____
_____
_____
_____

What are some ways I can plant this truth deep in my heart?

_____
_____
_____
_____

What is going on in my life that I need to apply this verse to?

_____
_____
_____
_____

# Today's Verse

**Date**

## Ponder & Pray

Start with Worship. Tell the Lord how you feel about Him.
Thank Him for what this verse shows you about His nature.

_____

_____

_____

_____

Lord, what do you have to say to me through this verse?

_____

_____

_____

_____

What are some ways I can plant this truth deep in my heart?

_____

_____

_____

_____

What is going on in my life that I need to apply this verse to?

_____

_____

_____

_____

**Date**

*Today's Verse*

*Ponder & Pray*

Start with Worship. Tell the Lord how you feel about Him.
Thank Him for what this verse shows you about His nature.

_____

_____

_____

_____

Lord, what do you have to say to me through this verse?

_____

_____

_____

_____

What are some ways I can plant this truth deep in my heart?

_____

_____

_____

_____

What is going on in my life that I need to apply this verse to?

_____

_____

_____

_____

## Today's Verse

**Date**

### Ponder & Pray

Start with Worship. Tell the Lord how you feel about Him. Thank Him for what this verse shows you about His nature.

_____
_____
_____
_____

Lord, what do you have to say to me through this verse?

_____
_____
_____
_____

What are some ways I can plant this truth deep in my heart?

_____
_____
_____
_____

What is going on in my life that I need to apply this verse to?

_____
_____
_____
_____

**Date**

## Today's Verse

### Ponder & Pray

START WITH WORSHIP. TELL THE LORD HOW YOU FEEL ABOUT HIM.
THANK HIM FOR WHAT THIS VERSE SHOWS YOU ABOUT HIS NATURE.

_____

_____

_____

_____

LORD, WHAT DO YOU HAVE TO SAY TO ME THROUGH THIS VERSE?

_____

_____

_____

_____

WHAT ARE SOME WAYS I CAN PLANT THIS TRUTH DEEP IN MY HEART?

_____

_____

_____

_____

WHAT IS GOING ON IN MY LIFE THAT I NEED TO APPLY THIS VERSE TO?

_____

_____

_____

_____

# Journal

Take time to sit, rest, breathe...be before the Lord.
What does he have to say to you?

Date

*Dwell*

"MAY YOUR UNFAILING LOVE COME TO ME, LORD, YOUR SALVATION, ACCORDING TO YOUR PROMISE"

*Psalm 119:41 Niv*

22

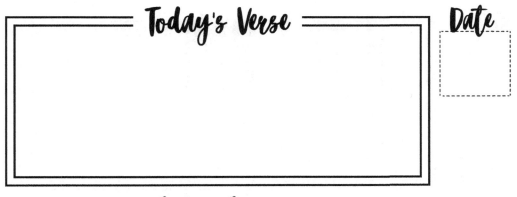

## Ponder & Pray

Start with Worship. Tell the Lord how you feel about Him. Thank Him for what this verse shows you about His nature.

_____
_____
_____
_____

Lord, what do you have to say to me through this verse?

_____
_____
_____
_____

What are some ways I can plant this truth deep in my heart?

_____
_____
_____
_____

What is going on in my life that I need to apply this verse to?

_____
_____
_____
_____

**Date**

## Today's Verse

### Ponder & Pray

START WITH WORSHIP. TELL THE LORD HOW YOU FEEL ABOUT HIM.
THANK HIM FOR WHAT THIS VERSE SHOWS YOU ABOUT HIS NATURE.

_____
_____
_____
_____

LORD, WHAT DO YOU HAVE TO SAY TO ME THROUGH THIS VERSE?

_____
_____
_____
_____

WHAT ARE SOME WAYS I CAN PLANT THIS TRUTH DEEP IN MY HEART?

_____
_____
_____
_____
_____

WHAT IS GOING ON IN MY LIFE THAT I NEED TO APPLY THIS VERSE TO?

_____
_____
_____
_____

## Today's Verse

### Date

## Ponder & Pray

START WITH WORSHIP. TELL THE LORD HOW YOU FEEL ABOUT HIM.
THANK HIM FOR WHAT THIS VERSE SHOWS YOU ABOUT HIS NATURE.

_____

_____

_____

_____

LORD, WHAT DO YOU HAVE TO SAY TO ME THROUGH THIS VERSE?

_____

_____

_____

_____

WHAT ARE SOME WAYS I CAN PLANT THIS TRUTH DEEP IN MY HEART?

_____

_____

_____

_____

WHAT IS GOING ON IN MY LIFE THAT I NEED TO APPLY THIS VERSE TO?

_____

_____

_____

_____

## Date

## Today's Verse

### Ponder & Pray

Start with Worship. Tell the Lord how you feel about Him.
Thank Him for what this verse shows you about His nature.

_____

_____

_____

_____

Lord, what do you have to say to me through this verse?

_____

_____

_____

_____

What are some ways I can plant this truth deep in my heart?

_____

_____

_____

_____

What is going on in my life that I need to apply this verse to?

_____

_____

_____

_____

# Today's Verse

## Ponder & Pray

Start with Worship. Tell the Lord how you feel about Him. Thank Him for what this verse shows you about His nature.

_____
_____
_____
_____

Lord, what do you have to say to me through this verse?

_____
_____
_____
_____

What are some ways I can plant this truth deep in my heart?

_____
_____
_____
_____
_____

What is going on in my life that I need to apply this verse to?

_____
_____
_____
_____
_____

# Today's Verse

## Ponder & Pray

Start with Worship. Tell the Lord how you feel about Him. Thank Him for what this verse shows you about His nature.

_____

_____

_____

Lord, what do you have to say to me through this verse?

_____

_____

_____

What are some ways I can plant this truth deep in my heart?

_____

_____

_____

What is going on in my life that I need to apply this verse to?

_____

_____

_____

# Journal

Take time to sit, rest, breathe...be before the Lord.
What does he have to say to you?

Date

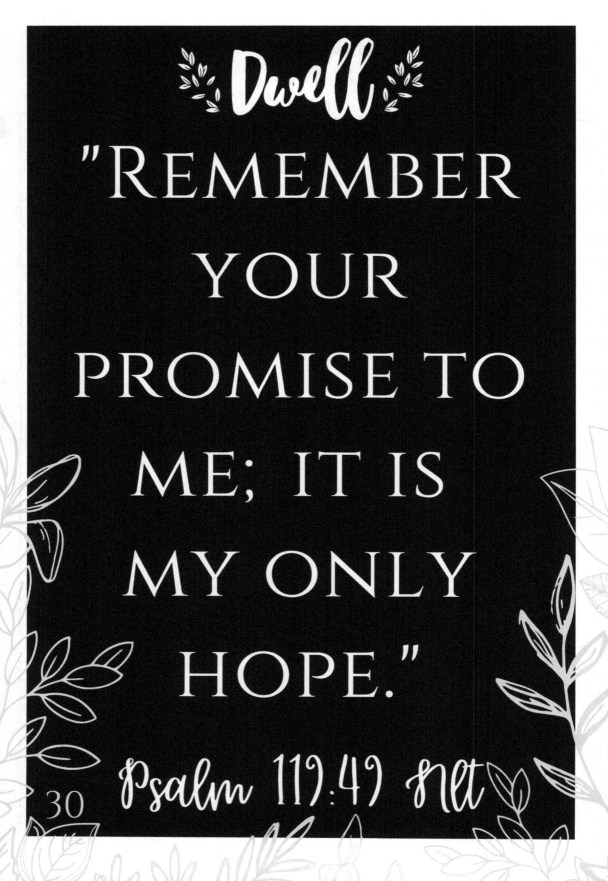

Dwell

"REMEMBER YOUR PROMISE TO ME; IT IS MY ONLY HOPE."

Psalm 119:49 NET

30

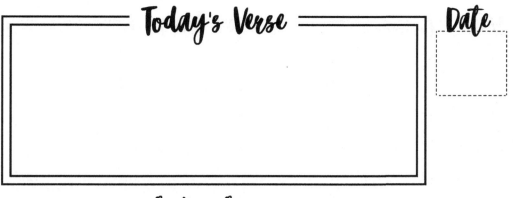

# Today's Verse

**Date**

## Ponder & Pray

Start with Worship. Tell the Lord how you feel about Him.
Thank Him for what this verse shows you about His nature.

_____
_____
_____
_____

Lord, what do you have to say to me through this verse?

_____
_____
_____
_____

What are some ways I can plant this truth deep in my heart?

_____
_____
_____
_____

What is going on in my life that I need to apply this verse to?

_____
_____
_____
_____

**Date**

## Today's Verse

### Ponder & Pray

Start with Worship. Tell the Lord how you feel about Him.
Thank Him for what this verse shows you about His nature.

_____

_____

_____

_____

Lord, what do you have to say to me through this verse?

_____

_____

_____

_____

What are some ways I can plant this truth deep in my heart?

_____

_____

_____

_____

What is going on in my life that I need to apply this verse to?

_____

_____

_____

_____

## Today's Verse

### Date

## Ponder & Pray

START WITH WORSHIP. TELL THE LORD HOW YOU FEEL ABOUT HIM.
THANK HIM FOR WHAT THIS VERSE SHOWS YOU ABOUT HIS NATURE.

_____
_____
_____
_____

LORD, WHAT DO YOU HAVE TO SAY TO ME THROUGH THIS VERSE?

_____
_____
_____
_____

WHAT ARE SOME WAYS I CAN PLANT THIS TRUTH DEEP IN MY HEART?

_____
_____
_____
_____

WHAT IS GOING ON IN MY LIFE THAT I NEED TO APPLY THIS VERSE TO?

_____
_____
_____
_____

**Date**

## Today's Verse

### Ponder & Pray

Start with Worship. Tell the Lord how you feel about Him.
Thank Him for what this verse shows you about His nature.

_____
_____
_____
_____

Lord, what do you have to say to me through this verse?

_____
_____
_____
_____

What are some ways I can plant this truth deep in my heart?

_____
_____
_____
_____

What is going on in my life that I need to apply this verse to?

_____
_____
_____
_____

## Today's Verse

### Date

## Ponder & Pray

Start with Worship.  Tell the Lord how you feel about Him.
Thank Him for what this verse shows you about His nature.

_____

_____

_____

_____

Lord, what do you have to say to me through this verse?

_____

_____

_____

_____

What are some ways I can plant this truth deep in my heart?

_____

_____

_____

_____

What is going on in my life that I need to apply this verse to?

_____

_____

_____

_____

**Date**

## Today's Verse

## Ponder & Pray

Start with Worship. Tell the Lord how you feel about Him. Thank Him for what this verse shows you about His nature.

_____

_____

_____

_____

Lord, what do you have to say to me through this verse?

_____

_____

_____

_____

What are some ways I can plant this truth deep in my heart?

_____

_____

_____

_____

What is going on in my life that I need to apply this verse to?

_____

_____

_____

_____

# Journal

Take time to sit, rest, breathe...be before the Lord.
What does he have to say to you?

Date

# Dwell

"I HAVE SOUGHT YOUR FACE WITH ALL MY HEART; BE GRACIOUS TO ME ACCORDING TO YOUR PROMISE."

Psalm 119:58 Niv

38

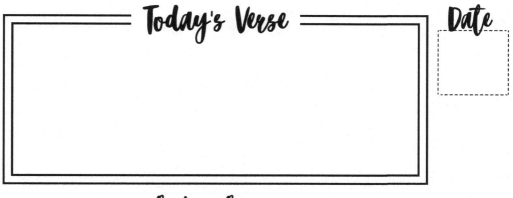

# Today's Verse

## Date

## Ponder & Pray

Start with Worship. Tell the Lord how you feel about Him. Thank Him for what this verse shows you about His nature.

_____
_____
_____
_____

Lord, what do you have to say to me through this verse?

_____
_____
_____
_____

What are some ways I can plant this truth deep in my heart?

_____
_____
_____
_____

What is going on in my life that I need to apply this verse to?

_____
_____
_____
_____

**Date**

## Today's Verse

### Ponder & Pray

Start with Worship. Tell the Lord how you feel about Him.
Thank Him for what this verse shows you about His nature.

_____
_____
_____
_____

Lord, what do you have to say to me through this verse?

_____
_____
_____
_____

What are some ways I can plant this truth deep in my heart?

_____
_____
_____
_____
_____

What is going on in my life that I need to apply this verse to?

_____
_____
_____
_____

# Today's Verse

## Date

## Ponder & Pray

Start with Worship. Tell the Lord how you feel about Him. Thank Him for what this verse shows you about His nature.

_____

_____

_____

_____

Lord, what do you have to say to me through this verse?

_____

_____

_____

_____

What are some ways I can plant this truth deep in my heart?

_____

_____

_____

_____

What is going on in my life that I need to apply this verse to?

_____

_____

_____

_____

**Date**

## Today's Verse

### Ponder & Pray

START WITH WORSHIP. TELL THE LORD HOW YOU FEEL ABOUT HIM.
THANK HIM FOR WHAT THIS VERSE SHOWS YOU ABOUT HIS NATURE.

_____

_____

_____

_____

LORD, WHAT DO YOU HAVE TO SAY TO ME THROUGH THIS VERSE?

_____

_____

_____

_____

WHAT ARE SOME WAYS I CAN PLANT THIS TRUTH DEEP IN MY HEART?

_____

_____

_____

_____

_____

WHAT IS GOING ON IN MY LIFE THAT I NEED TO APPLY THIS VERSE TO?

_____

_____

_____

_____

_____

# Today's Verse

### Date

## Ponder & Pray

START WITH WORSHIP. TELL THE LORD HOW YOU FEEL ABOUT HIM.
THANK HIM FOR WHAT THIS VERSE SHOWS YOU ABOUT HIS NATURE.

_____
_____
_____

LORD, WHAT DO YOU HAVE TO SAY TO ME THROUGH THIS VERSE?

_____
_____
_____

WHAT ARE SOME WAYS I CAN PLANT THIS TRUTH DEEP IN MY HEART?

_____
_____
_____

WHAT IS GOING ON IN MY LIFE THAT I NEED TO APPLY THIS VERSE TO?

_____
_____
_____

**Date**

## Today's Verse

### Ponder & Pray

Start with Worship. Tell the Lord how you feel about Him.
Thank Him for what this verse shows you about His nature.

_____
_____
_____
_____

Lord, what do you have to say to me through this verse?

_____
_____
_____
_____

What are some ways I can plant this truth deep in my heart?

_____
_____
_____
_____

What is going on in my life that I need to apply this verse to?

_____
_____
_____
_____

# Journal

Take time to sit, rest, breathe...be before the Lord.
WHAT DOES HE HAVE TO SAY TO YOU?

Date

# Dwell

"YOUR WORD, LORD, IS ETERNAL; IT STANDS FIRM IN THE HEAVENS."

Psalm 119:89 Niv

46

# Today's Verse

## Ponder & Pray

Start with Worship. Tell the Lord how you feel about Him.
Thank Him for what this verse shows you about His nature.

_____
_____
_____
_____

Lord, what do you have to say to me through this verse?

_____
_____
_____
_____
_____

What are some ways I can plant this truth deep in my heart?

_____
_____
_____
_____
_____

What is going on in my life that I need to apply this verse to?

_____
_____
_____
_____
_____

**Date**

## Today's Verse

### Ponder & Pray

Start with Worship.  Tell the Lord how you feel about Him.
Thank Him for what this verse shows you about His nature.

_____

_____

_____

Lord, what do you have to say to me through this verse?

_____

_____

_____

What are some ways I can plant this truth deep in my heart?

_____

_____

_____

_____

What is going on in my life that I need to apply this verse to?

_____

_____

_____

_____

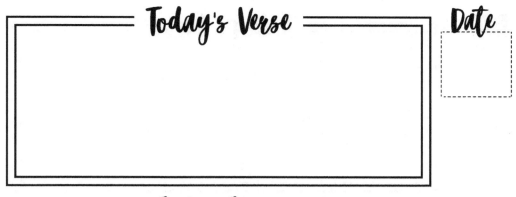

## Today's Verse

**Date**

### Ponder & Pray

Start with Worship. Tell the Lord how you feel about Him.
Thank Him for what this verse shows you about His nature.

_____
_____
_____
_____

Lord, what do you have to say to me through this verse?

_____
_____
_____
_____

What are some ways I can plant this truth deep in my heart?

_____
_____
_____
_____

What is going on in my life that I need to apply this verse to?

_____
_____
_____
_____

**Date**

## Today's Verse

### Ponder & Pray

START WITH WORSHIP. TELL THE LORD HOW YOU FEEL ABOUT HIM.
THANK HIM FOR WHAT THIS VERSE SHOWS YOU ABOUT HIS NATURE.

_____

_____

_____

_____

LORD, WHAT DO YOU HAVE TO SAY TO ME THROUGH THIS VERSE?

_____

_____

_____

_____

WHAT ARE SOME WAYS I CAN PLANT THIS TRUTH DEEP IN MY HEART?

_____

_____

_____

_____

WHAT IS GOING ON IN MY LIFE THAT I NEED TO APPLY THIS VERSE TO?

_____

_____

_____

_____

# Today's Verse

## Ponder & Pray

Start with Worship. Tell the Lord how you feel about Him.
Thank Him for what this verse shows you about His nature.

_____

_____

_____

_____

Lord, what do you have to say to me through this verse?

_____

_____

_____

_____

What are some ways I can plant this truth deep in my heart?

_____

_____

_____

_____

What is going on in my life that I need to apply this verse to?

_____

_____

_____

_____

## Date

## Today's Verse

## Ponder & Pray

Start with Worship. Tell the Lord how you feel about Him.
Thank Him for what this verse shows you about His nature.

_____
_____
_____

Lord, what do you have to say to me through this verse?

_____
_____
_____

What are some ways I can plant this truth deep in my heart?

_____
_____
_____
_____

What is going on in my life that I need to apply this verse to?

_____
_____
_____
_____

# Journal

Date

Take time to sit, rest, breathe...be before the Lord.
WHAT DOES HE HAVE TO SAY TO YOU?

# Dwell

"OH, HOW I LOVE YOUR LAW! I MEDITATE ON IT ALL DAY LONG."

Psalm 119:97 NIV

# Today's Verse

**Date**

## Ponder & Pray

START WITH WORSHIP. TELL THE LORD HOW YOU FEEL ABOUT HIM.
THANK HIM FOR WHAT THIS VERSE SHOWS YOU ABOUT HIS NATURE.

LORD, WHAT DO YOU HAVE TO SAY TO ME THROUGH THIS VERSE?

WHAT ARE SOME WAYS I CAN PLANT THIS TRUTH DEEP IN MY HEART?

WHAT IS GOING ON IN MY LIFE THAT I NEED TO APPLY THIS VERSE TO?

**Date**

## Today's Verse

### Ponder & Pray

Start with Worship. Tell the Lord how you feel about Him. Thank Him for what this verse shows you about His nature.

_____
_____
_____

Lord, what do you have to say to me through this verse?

_____
_____
_____

What are some ways I can plant this truth deep in my heart?

_____
_____
_____
_____

What is going on in my life that I need to apply this verse to?

_____
_____
_____
_____
_____

## Today's Verse

**Date**

### Ponder & Pray

Start with Worship. Tell the Lord how you feel about Him.
Thank Him for what this verse shows you about His nature.

_____
_____
_____
_____

Lord, what do you have to say to me through this verse?

_____
_____
_____
_____

What are some ways I can plant this truth deep in my heart?

_____
_____
_____
_____

What is going on in my life that I need to apply this verse to?

_____
_____
_____
_____

**Date**

## Today's Verse

### Ponder & Pray

Start with Worship. Tell the Lord how you feel about Him.
Thank Him for what this verse shows you about His nature.

_____
_____
_____
_____

Lord, what do you have to say to me through this verse?

_____
_____
_____
_____

What are some ways I can plant this truth deep in my heart?

_____
_____
_____
_____

What is going on in my life that I need to apply this verse to?

_____
_____
_____
_____

## Today's Verse

### Date

### Ponder & Pray

Start with Worship. Tell the Lord how you feel about Him. Thank Him for what this verse shows you about His nature.

_____
_____
_____
_____

Lord, what do you have to say to me through this verse?

_____
_____
_____
_____

What are some ways I can plant this truth deep in my heart?

_____
_____
_____
_____

What is going on in my life that I need to apply this verse to?

_____
_____
_____
_____

**Date**

## Today's Verse

### Ponder & Pray

START WITH WORSHIP. TELL THE LORD HOW YOU FEEL ABOUT HIM.
THANK HIM FOR WHAT THIS VERSE SHOWS YOU ABOUT HIS NATURE.

_____

_____

_____

LORD, WHAT DO YOU HAVE TO SAY TO ME THROUGH THIS VERSE?

_____

_____

_____

WHAT ARE SOME WAYS I CAN PLANT THIS TRUTH DEEP IN MY HEART?

_____

_____

_____

WHAT IS GOING ON IN MY LIFE THAT I NEED TO APPLY THIS VERSE TO?

_____

_____

_____

_____

# Journal

Date

Take time to sit, rest, breathe...be before the Lord.
What does he have to say to you?

# Dwell

## "HOW SWEET ARE YOUR WORDS TO MY TASTE, SWEETER THAN HONEY TO MY MOUTH!"

*Psalm 119:103 Niv*

62

## Today's Verse

## Date

### Ponder & Pray

START WITH WORSHIP. TELL THE LORD HOW YOU FEEL ABOUT HIM.
THANK HIM FOR WHAT THIS VERSE SHOWS YOU ABOUT HIS NATURE.

_____
_____
_____

_____

LORD, WHAT DO YOU HAVE TO SAY TO ME THROUGH THIS VERSE?

_____
_____
_____

_____

WHAT ARE SOME WAYS I CAN PLANT THIS TRUTH DEEP IN MY HEART?

_____
_____
_____

_____

WHAT IS GOING ON IN MY LIFE THAT I NEED TO APPLY THIS VERSE TO?

_____
_____
_____
_____
_____

**Date**

## Today's Verse

### Ponder & Pray

Start with Worship. Tell the Lord how you feel about Him.
Thank Him for what this verse shows you about His nature.

_____

_____

_____

_____

Lord, what do you have to say to me through this verse?

_____

_____

_____

_____

What are some ways I can plant this truth deep in my heart?

_____

_____

_____

_____

_____

What is going on in my life that I need to apply this verse to?

_____

_____

_____

_____

_____

## Today's Verse

**Date**

### Ponder & Pray

START WITH WORSHIP. TELL THE LORD HOW YOU FEEL ABOUT HIM.
THANK HIM FOR WHAT THIS VERSE SHOWS YOU ABOUT HIS NATURE.

LORD, WHAT DO YOU HAVE TO SAY TO ME THROUGH THIS VERSE?

WHAT ARE SOME WAYS I CAN PLANT THIS TRUTH DEEP IN MY HEART?

WHAT IS GOING ON IN MY LIFE THAT I NEED TO APPLY THIS VERSE TO?

**Date**

## Today's Verse

## Ponder & Pray

START WITH WORSHIP. TELL THE LORD HOW YOU FEEL ABOUT HIM.
THANK HIM FOR WHAT THIS VERSE SHOWS YOU ABOUT HIS NATURE.

_____
_____
_____
_____

LORD, WHAT DO YOU HAVE TO SAY TO ME THROUGH THIS VERSE?

_____
_____
_____
_____

WHAT ARE SOME WAYS I CAN PLANT THIS TRUTH DEEP IN MY HEART?

_____
_____
_____
_____

WHAT IS GOING ON IN MY LIFE THAT I NEED TO APPLY THIS VERSE TO?

_____
_____
_____
_____

# Today's Verse

## Ponder & Pray

START WITH WORSHIP. TELL THE LORD HOW YOU FEEL ABOUT HIM.
THANK HIM FOR WHAT THIS VERSE SHOWS YOU ABOUT HIS NATURE.

_____

_____

_____

_____

LORD, WHAT DO YOU HAVE TO SAY TO ME THROUGH THIS VERSE?

_____

_____

_____

_____

WHAT ARE SOME WAYS I CAN PLANT THIS TRUTH DEEP IN MY HEART?

_____

_____

_____

_____

WHAT IS GOING ON IN MY LIFE THAT I NEED TO APPLY THIS VERSE TO?

_____

_____

_____

_____

**Date**

# Today's Verse

## Ponder & Pray

Start with Worship. Tell the Lord how you feel about Him.
Thank Him for what this verse shows you about His nature.

_____

_____

_____

_____

Lord, what do you have to say to me through this verse?

_____

_____

_____

_____

What are some ways I can plant this truth deep in my heart?

_____

_____

_____

_____

What is going on in my life that I need to apply this verse to?

_____

_____

_____

_____

# Journal

TAKE TIME TO SIT, REST, BREATHE...BE BEFORE THE LORD.
WHAT DOES HE HAVE TO SAY TO YOU?

# Dwell

"Your word is a lamp for my feet, a light on my path."

Psalm 119:105 Niv

# Today's Verse

## Ponder & Pray

Start with Worship. Tell the Lord how you feel about Him. Thank Him for what this verse shows you about His nature.

_____

_____

_____

_____

Lord, what do you have to say to me through this verse?

_____

_____

_____

_____

What are some ways I can plant this truth deep in my heart?

_____

_____

_____

_____

What is going on in my life that I need to apply this verse to?

_____

_____

_____

_____

**Date**

## Today's Verse

### Ponder & Pray

Start with Worship. Tell the Lord how you feel about Him.
Thank Him for what this verse shows you about His nature.

_____

_____

_____

_____

Lord, what do you have to say to me through this verse?

_____

_____

_____

_____

What are some ways I can plant this truth deep in my heart?

_____

_____

_____

_____

What is going on in my life that I need to apply this verse to?

_____

_____

_____

_____

_____

## Today's Verse

**Date**

### Ponder & Pray

Start with Worship. Tell the Lord how you feel about Him.
Thank Him for what this verse shows you about His nature.

_____

_____

_____

_____

Lord, what do you have to say to me through this verse?

_____

_____

_____

_____

What are some ways I can plant this truth deep in my heart?

_____

_____

_____

_____

What is going on in my life that I need to apply this verse to?

_____

_____

_____

_____

Date

Today's Verse

## Ponder & Pray

Start with Worship. Tell the Lord how you feel about Him.
Thank Him for what this verse shows you about His nature.

_____
_____
_____
_____

Lord, what do you have to say to me through this verse?

_____
_____
_____
_____

What are some ways I can plant this truth deep in my heart?

_____
_____
_____
_____

What is going on in my life that I need to apply this verse to?

_____
_____
_____
_____

# Today's Verse

Date

## Ponder & Pray

Start with Worship. Tell the Lord how you feel about Him.
Thank Him for what this verse shows you about His nature.

_____

_____

_____

Lord, what do you have to say to me through this verse?

_____

_____

_____

What are some ways I can plant this truth deep in my heart?

_____

_____

_____

What is going on in my life that I need to apply this verse to?

_____

_____

_____

_____

## Date

## Today's Verse

## Ponder & Pray

Start with Worship. Tell the Lord how you feel about Him.
Thank Him for what this verse shows you about His nature.

_____

_____

_____

_____

Lord, what do you have to say to me through this verse?

_____

_____

_____

_____

What are some ways I can plant this truth deep in my heart?

_____

_____

_____

_____

What is going on in my life that I need to apply this verse to?

_____

_____

_____

_____

# Journal

Date

TAKE TIME TO SIT, REST, BREATHE...BE BEFORE THE LORD.
WHAT DOES HE HAVE TO SAY TO YOU?

# Dwell

"YOUR LAWS
ARE MY
TREASURE;
THEY ARE
MY HEART'S
DELIGHT."

*Psalm 119:111 Niv*

# Today's Verse

### Date

## Ponder & Pray

START WITH WORSHIP. TELL THE LORD HOW YOU FEEL ABOUT HIM.
THANK HIM FOR WHAT THIS VERSE SHOWS YOU ABOUT HIS NATURE.

_____

_____

_____

_____

LORD, WHAT DO YOU HAVE TO SAY TO ME THROUGH THIS VERSE?

_____

_____

_____

_____

WHAT ARE SOME WAYS I CAN PLANT THIS TRUTH DEEP IN MY HEART?

_____

_____

_____

_____

WHAT IS GOING ON IN MY LIFE THAT I NEED TO APPLY THIS VERSE TO?

_____

_____

_____

_____

**Date**

## Today's Verse

### Ponder & Pray

Start with Worship. Tell the Lord how you feel about Him.
Thank Him for what this verse shows you about His nature.

_____
_____
_____
_____

Lord, what do you have to say to me through this verse?

_____
_____
_____
_____

What are some ways I can plant this truth deep in my heart?

_____
_____
_____
_____

What is going on in my life that I need to apply this verse to?

_____
_____
_____
_____

## Today's Verse

### Date

## Ponder & Pray

START WITH WORSHIP. TELL THE LORD HOW YOU FEEL ABOUT HIM.
THANK HIM FOR WHAT THIS VERSE SHOWS YOU ABOUT HIS NATURE.

_____

_____

_____

LORD, WHAT DO YOU HAVE TO SAY TO ME THROUGH THIS VERSE?

_____

_____

_____

WHAT ARE SOME WAYS I CAN PLANT THIS TRUTH DEEP IN MY HEART?

_____

_____

_____

WHAT IS GOING ON IN MY LIFE THAT I NEED TO APPLY THIS VERSE TO?

_____

_____

_____

**Date**

## Today's Verse

### Ponder & Pray

Start with Worship. Tell the Lord how you feel about Him.
Thank Him for what this verse shows you about His nature.

_____

_____

_____

_____

Lord, what do you have to say to me through this verse?

_____

_____

_____

_____

What are some ways I can plant this truth deep in my heart?

_____

_____

_____

_____

What is going on in my life that I need to apply this verse to?

_____

_____

_____

_____

# Today's Verse

## Ponder & Pray

Start with Worship. Tell the Lord how you feel about Him.
Thank Him for what this verse shows you about His nature.

_____
_____
_____
_____

Lord, what do you have to say to me through this verse?

_____
_____
_____
_____

What are some ways I can plant this truth deep in my heart?

_____
_____
_____
_____
_____

What is going on in my life that I need to apply this verse to?

_____
_____
_____
_____

**Date**

# Today's Verse

## Ponder & Pray

Start with Worship. Tell the Lord how you feel about Him.
Thank Him for what this verse shows you about His nature.

_____

_____

_____

_____

Lord, what do you have to say to me through this verse?

_____

_____

_____

_____

What are some ways I can plant this truth deep in my heart?

_____

_____

_____

_____

What is going on in my life that I need to apply this verse to?

_____

_____

_____

_____

# Journal

Take time to sit, rest, breathe...be before the Lord.
What does he have to say to you?

# Dwell

"Sustain me, my God, according to your promise, and I will live"

*Psalm 119:116a Niv*

86

# Today's Verse

## Ponder & Pray

START WITH WORSHIP. TELL THE LORD HOW YOU FEEL ABOUT HIM.
THANK HIM FOR WHAT THIS VERSE SHOWS YOU ABOUT HIS NATURE.

_____
_____
_____
_____

LORD, WHAT DO YOU HAVE TO SAY TO ME THROUGH THIS VERSE?

_____
_____
_____
_____

WHAT ARE SOME WAYS I CAN PLANT THIS TRUTH DEEP IN MY HEART?

_____
_____
_____
_____

WHAT IS GOING ON IN MY LIFE THAT I NEED TO APPLY THIS VERSE TO?

_____
_____
_____
_____

Date

## Today's Verse

## Ponder & Pray

Start with Worship. Tell the Lord how you feel about Him.
Thank Him for what this verse shows you about His nature.

_____

_____

_____

_____

Lord, what do you have to say to me through this verse?

_____

_____

_____

_____

What are some ways I can plant this truth deep in my heart?

_____

_____

_____

_____

What is going on in my life that I need to apply this verse to?

_____

_____

_____

_____

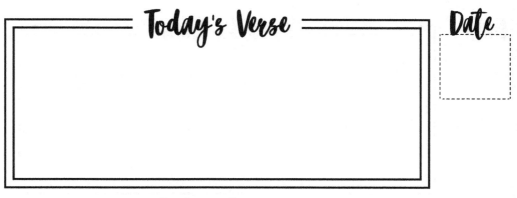

## Today's Verse

### Date

## Ponder & Pray

Start with Worship. Tell the Lord how you feel about Him.
Thank Him for what this verse shows you about His nature.

_____

_____

_____

_____

Lord, what do you have to say to me through this verse?

_____

_____

_____

_____

What are some ways I can plant this truth deep in my heart?

_____

_____

_____

_____

_____

What is going on in my life that I need to apply this verse to?

_____

_____

_____

_____

**Date**

## Today's Verse

### Ponder & Pray

Start with Worship. Tell the Lord how you feel about Him.
Thank Him for what this verse shows you about His nature.

_____

_____

_____

_____

Lord, what do you have to say to me through this verse?

_____

_____

_____

_____

What are some ways I can plant this truth deep in my heart?

_____

_____

_____

_____

_____

What is going on in my life that I need to apply this verse to?

_____

_____

_____

_____

# Today's Verse

## Ponder & Pray

Start with Worship. Tell the Lord how you feel about Him.
Thank Him for what this verse shows you about His nature.

_____
_____
_____
_____

Lord, what do you have to say to me through this verse?

_____
_____
_____
_____

What are some ways I can plant this truth deep in my heart?

_____
_____
_____
_____

What is going on in my life that I need to apply this verse to?

_____
_____
_____
_____

**Date**

## Today's Verse

### Ponder & Pray

Start with Worship. Tell the Lord how you feel about Him.
Thank Him for what this verse shows you about His nature.

_____

_____

_____

_____

Lord, what do you have to say to me through this verse?

_____

_____

_____

_____

What are some ways I can plant this truth deep in my heart?

_____

_____

_____

_____

What is going on in my life that I need to apply this verse to?

_____

_____

_____

# Journal

Date

Take time to sit, rest, breathe...be before the Lord.
What does he have to say to you?

*Dwell*

"DIRECT MY FOOTSTEPS ACCORDING TO YOUR WORD; LET NO SIN RULE OVER ME."

*Psalm 119:133 Niv*

94

# Today's Verse

## Ponder & Pray

Start with Worship. Tell the Lord how you feel about Him. Thank Him for what this verse shows you about His nature.

_____
_____
_____
_____

Lord, what do you have to say to me through this verse?

_____
_____
_____
_____

What are some ways I can plant this truth deep in my heart?

_____
_____
_____
_____

What is going on in my life that I need to apply this verse to?

_____
_____
_____
_____

**Date**

## Today's Verse

## Ponder & Pray

Start with Worship. Tell the Lord how you feel about Him.
Thank Him for what this verse shows you about His nature.

_____

_____

_____

_____

Lord, what do you have to say to me through this verse?

_____

_____

_____

_____

What are some ways I can plant this truth deep in my heart?

_____

_____

_____

_____

What is going on in my life that I need to apply this verse to?

_____

_____

_____

_____

## Today's Verse

**Date**

### Ponder & Pray

Start with Worship. Tell the Lord how you feel about Him. Thank Him for what this verse shows you about His nature.

_____
_____
_____
_____

Lord, what do you have to say to me through this verse?

_____
_____
_____
_____

What are some ways I can plant this truth deep in my heart?

_____
_____
_____
_____

What is going on in my life that I need to apply this verse to?

_____
_____
_____
_____

**Date**

## Today's Verse

## Ponder & Pray

Start with Worship. Tell the Lord how you feel about Him.
Thank Him for what this verse shows you about His nature.

_____
_____
_____
_____

Lord, what do you have to say to me through this verse?

_____
_____
_____
_____

What are some ways I can plant this truth deep in my heart?

_____
_____
_____
_____

What is going on in my life that I need to apply this verse to?

_____
_____
_____
_____

# Today's Verse

## Ponder & Pray

START WITH WORSHIP. TELL THE LORD HOW YOU FEEL ABOUT HIM.
THANK HIM FOR WHAT THIS VERSE SHOWS YOU ABOUT HIS NATURE.

_____
_____
_____
_____

LORD, WHAT DO YOU HAVE TO SAY TO ME THROUGH THIS VERSE?

_____
_____
_____
_____

WHAT ARE SOME WAYS I CAN PLANT THIS TRUTH DEEP IN MY HEART?

_____
_____
_____
_____

WHAT IS GOING ON IN MY LIFE THAT I NEED TO APPLY THIS VERSE TO?

_____
_____
_____
_____

**Date**

## Today's Verse

### Ponder & Pray

Start with Worship. Tell the Lord how you feel about Him.
Thank Him for what this verse shows you about His nature.

_____

_____

_____

_____

Lord, what do you have to say to me through this verse?

_____

_____

_____

_____

What are some ways I can plant this truth deep in my heart?

_____

_____

_____

_____

What is going on in my life that I need to apply this verse to?

_____

_____

_____

_____

# Journal

Date

TAKE TIME TO SIT, REST, BREATHE...BE BEFORE THE LORD.
WHAT DOES HE HAVE TO SAY TO YOU?

## Dwell

"I RISE BEFORE DAWN AND CRY FOR HELP; I HAVE PUT MY HOPE IN YOUR WORD."

Psalm 119:47 Niv

# Today's Verse

## Date

## Ponder & Pray

Start with Worship. Tell the Lord how you feel about Him. Thank Him for what this verse shows you about His nature.

_____
_____
_____
_____

Lord, what do you have to say to me through this verse?

_____
_____
_____
_____

What are some ways I can plant this truth deep in my heart?

_____
_____
_____
_____

What is going on in my life that I need to apply this verse to?

_____
_____
_____
_____

## Date

## Today's Verse

### Ponder & Pray

Start with Worship. Tell the Lord how you feel about Him. Thank Him for what this verse shows you about His nature.

_____

_____

_____

_____

Lord, what do you have to say to me through this verse?

_____

_____

_____

_____

What are some ways I can plant this truth deep in my heart?

_____

_____

_____

_____

What is going on in my life that I need to apply this verse to?

_____

_____

_____

_____

## Today's Verse

**Date**

## Ponder & Pray

Start with Worship. Tell the Lord how you feel about Him.
Thank Him for what this verse shows you about His nature.

_____

_____

_____

Lord, what do you have to say to me through this verse?

_____

_____

_____

_____

What are some ways I can plant this truth deep in my heart?

_____

_____

_____

_____

What is going on in my life that I need to apply this verse to?

_____

_____

_____

_____

## Date

## Today's Verse

### Ponder & Pray

Start with Worship. Tell the Lord how you feel about Him.
Thank Him for what this verse shows you about His nature.

_____

_____

_____

_____

Lord, what do you have to say to me through this verse?

_____

_____

_____

_____

What are some ways I can plant this truth deep in my heart?

_____

_____

_____

_____

What is going on in my life that I need to apply this verse to?

_____

_____

_____

_____

# Today's Verse

## Ponder & Pray

START WITH WORSHIP. TELL THE LORD HOW YOU FEEL ABOUT HIM.
THANK HIM FOR WHAT THIS VERSE SHOWS YOU ABOUT HIS NATURE.

_____

_____

_____

_____

LORD, WHAT DO YOU HAVE TO SAY TO ME THROUGH THIS VERSE?

_____

_____

_____

_____

WHAT ARE SOME WAYS I CAN PLANT THIS TRUTH DEEP IN MY HEART?

_____

_____

_____

_____

WHAT IS GOING ON IN MY LIFE THAT I NEED TO APPLY THIS VERSE TO?

_____

_____

_____

_____

**Date**

## Today's Verse

### Ponder & Pray

Start with Worship. Tell the Lord how you feel about Him.
Thank Him for what this verse shows you about His nature.

_____

_____

_____

_____

Lord, what do you have to say to me through this verse?

_____

_____

_____

_____

What are some ways I can plant this truth deep in my heart?

_____

_____

_____

_____

What is going on in my life that I need to apply this verse to?

_____

_____

_____

_____

# Journal

TAKE TIME TO SIT, REST, BREATHE...BE BEFORE THE LORD.
WHAT DOES HE HAVE TO SAY TO YOU?

*Dwell*

"HEAR MY VOICE IN ACCORDANCE WITH YOUR LOVE; PRESERVE MY LIFE, LORD, ACCORDING TO YOUR LAWS."

Psalm 119:451 Niv

# Today's Verse

## Ponder & Pray

Start with Worship. Tell the Lord how you feel about Him.
Thank Him for what this verse shows you about His nature.

_____

_____

_____

_____

Lord, what do you have to say to me through this verse?

_____

_____

_____

_____

What are some ways I can plant this truth deep in my heart?

_____

_____

_____

_____

What is going on in my life that I need to apply this verse to?

_____

_____

_____

_____

**Date**

## Today's Verse

### Ponder & Pray

Start with Worship. Tell the Lord how you feel about Him. Thank Him for what this verse shows you about His nature.

_____
_____
_____

Lord, what do you have to say to me through this verse?

_____
_____
_____

What are some ways I can plant this truth deep in my heart?

_____
_____
_____

What is going on in my life that I need to apply this verse to?

_____
_____
_____

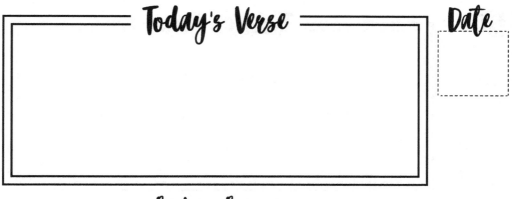

## Today's Verse

**Date**

## Ponder & Pray

START WITH WORSHIP. TELL THE LORD HOW YOU FEEL ABOUT HIM. THANK HIM FOR WHAT THIS VERSE SHOWS YOU ABOUT HIS NATURE.

_____
_____
_____
_____

LORD, WHAT DO YOU HAVE TO SAY TO ME THROUGH THIS VERSE?

_____
_____
_____
_____

WHAT ARE SOME WAYS I CAN PLANT THIS TRUTH DEEP IN MY HEART?

_____
_____
_____
_____

WHAT IS GOING ON IN MY LIFE THAT I NEED TO APPLY THIS VERSE TO?

_____
_____
_____
_____

**Date**

## Today's Verse

## Ponder & Pray

Start with Worship. Tell the Lord how you feel about Him.
Thank Him for what this verse shows you about His nature.

_____
_____
_____
_____

Lord, what do you have to say to me through this verse?

_____
_____
_____
_____

What are some ways I can plant this truth deep in my heart?

_____
_____
_____
_____

What is going on in my life that I need to apply this verse to?

_____
_____
_____
_____

# Today's Verse

## Ponder & Pray

Start with Worship. Tell the Lord how you feel about Him.
Thank Him for what this verse shows you about His nature.

_____

_____

_____

_____

Lord, what do you have to say to me through this verse?

_____

_____

_____

_____

What are some ways I can plant this truth deep in my heart?

_____

_____

_____

_____

What is going on in my life that I need to apply this verse to?

_____

_____

_____

_____

**Date**

## Today's Verse

## Ponder & Pray

Start with Worship. Tell the Lord how you feel about Him. Thank Him for what this verse shows you about His nature.

_____
_____
_____
_____

Lord, what do you have to say to me through this verse?

_____
_____
_____
_____

What are some ways I can plant this truth deep in my heart?

_____
_____
_____
_____

What is going on in my life that I need to apply this verse to?

_____
_____
_____
_____

# Journal

Take time to sit, rest, breathe...be before the Lord.
What does he have to say to you?

Date

# *Dwell*

"YET YOU ARE NEAR, LORD, AND ALL YOUR COMMANDS ARE TRUE."

*Psalm 119:151 Niv*

## Today's Verse

**Date**

### Ponder & Pray

START WITH WORSHIP. TELL THE LORD HOW YOU FEEL ABOUT HIM.
THANK HIM FOR WHAT THIS VERSE SHOWS YOU ABOUT HIS NATURE.

_____
_____
_____
_____

LORD, WHAT DO YOU HAVE TO SAY TO ME THROUGH THIS VERSE?

_____
_____
_____
_____

WHAT ARE SOME WAYS I CAN PLANT THIS TRUTH DEEP IN MY HEART?

_____
_____
_____
_____
_____

WHAT IS GOING ON IN MY LIFE THAT I NEED TO APPLY THIS VERSE TO?

_____
_____
_____
_____
_____

**Date**

## Today's Verse

### Ponder & Pray

START WITH WORSHIP. TELL THE LORD HOW YOU FEEL ABOUT HIM.
THANK HIM FOR WHAT THIS VERSE SHOWS YOU ABOUT HIS NATURE.

_____
_____
_____
_____

LORD, WHAT DO YOU HAVE TO SAY TO ME THROUGH THIS VERSE?

_____
_____
_____
_____

WHAT ARE SOME WAYS I CAN PLANT THIS TRUTH DEEP IN MY HEART?

_____
_____
_____
_____

WHAT IS GOING ON IN MY LIFE THAT I NEED TO APPLY THIS VERSE TO?

_____
_____
_____
_____

# Today's Verse

## Ponder & Pray

START WITH WORSHIP. TELL THE LORD HOW YOU FEEL ABOUT HIM.
THANK HIM FOR WHAT THIS VERSE SHOWS YOU ABOUT HIS NATURE.

_____

_____

_____

_____

LORD, WHAT DO YOU HAVE TO SAY TO ME THROUGH THIS VERSE?

_____

_____

_____

_____

WHAT ARE SOME WAYS I CAN PLANT THIS TRUTH DEEP IN MY HEART?

_____

_____

_____

_____

WHAT IS GOING ON IN MY LIFE THAT I NEED TO APPLY THIS VERSE TO?

_____

_____

_____

_____

**Date**

## Today's Verse

## Ponder & Pray

Start with Worship. Tell the Lord how you feel about Him.
Thank Him for what this verse shows you about His nature.

_____

_____

_____

_____

Lord, what do you have to say to me through this verse?

_____

_____

_____

_____

What are some ways I can plant this truth deep in my heart?

_____

_____

_____

_____

_____

What is going on in my life that I need to apply this verse to?

_____

_____

_____

_____

# Today's Verse

## Ponder & Pray

START WITH WORSHIP. TELL THE LORD HOW YOU FEEL ABOUT HIM.
THANK HIM FOR WHAT THIS VERSE SHOWS YOU ABOUT HIS NATURE.

_____

_____

_____

_____

LORD, WHAT DO YOU HAVE TO SAY TO ME THROUGH THIS VERSE?

_____

_____

_____

_____

WHAT ARE SOME WAYS I CAN PLANT THIS TRUTH DEEP IN MY HEART?

_____

_____

_____

_____

WHAT IS GOING ON IN MY LIFE THAT I NEED TO APPLY THIS VERSE TO?

_____

_____

_____

_____

**Date**

## Today's Verse

### Ponder & Pray

Start with Worship. Tell the Lord how you feel about Him. Thank Him for what this verse shows you about His nature.

_____
_____
_____
_____

Lord, what do you have to say to me through this verse?

_____
_____
_____
_____

What are some ways I can plant this truth deep in my heart?

_____
_____
_____
_____

What is going on in my life that I need to apply this verse to?

_____
_____
_____
_____

# Journal

TAKE TIME TO SIT, REST, BREATHE...BE BEFORE THE LORD.
WHAT DOES HE HAVE TO SAY TO YOU?

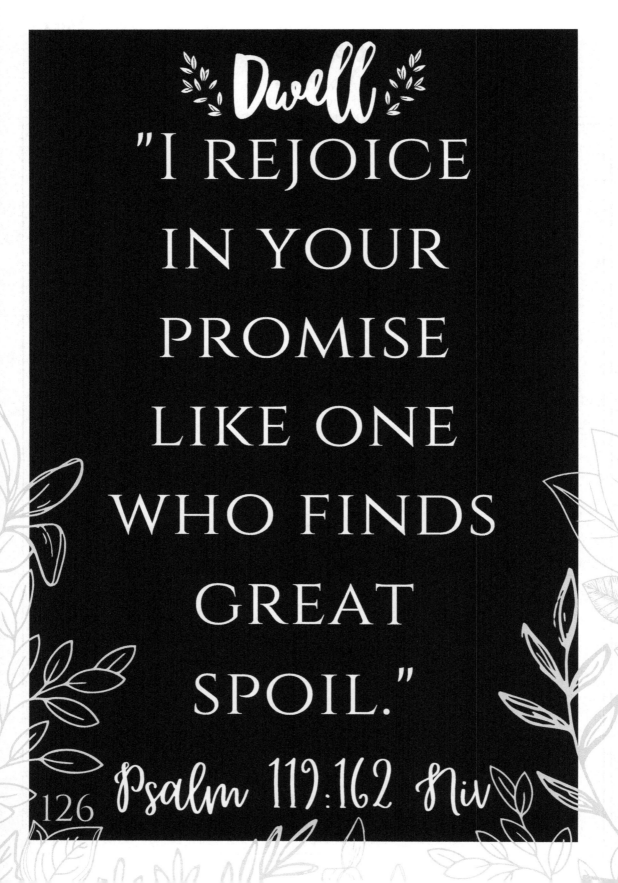

*Dwell*

"I REJOICE IN YOUR PROMISE LIKE ONE WHO FINDS GREAT SPOIL."

Psalm 119:162 Niv

126

# Today's Verse

## Date

## Ponder & Pray

Start with Worship. Tell the Lord how you feel about Him.
Thank Him for what this verse shows you about His nature.

_____

_____

_____

_____

Lord, what do you have to say to me through this verse?

_____

_____

_____

_____

What are some ways I can plant this truth deep in my heart?

_____

_____

_____

_____

What is going on in my life that I need to apply this verse to?

_____

_____

_____

_____

**Date**

## Today's Verse

### Ponder & Pray

Start with Worship. Tell the Lord how you feel about Him.
Thank Him for what this verse shows you about His nature.

_____
_____
_____
_____

Lord, what do you have to say to me through this verse?

_____
_____
_____
_____

What are some ways I can plant this truth deep in my heart?

_____
_____
_____
_____

What is going on in my life that I need to apply this verse to?

_____
_____
_____
_____

# Today's Verse

**Date**

## Ponder & Pray

Start with Worship. Tell the Lord how you feel about Him.
Thank Him for what this verse shows you about His nature.

_____

_____

_____

_____

Lord, what do you have to say to me through this verse?

_____

_____

_____

_____

What are some ways I can plant this truth deep in my heart?

_____

_____

_____

_____

What is going on in my life that I need to apply this verse to?

_____

_____

_____

_____

**Date**

## Today's Verse

### Ponder & Pray

Start with Worship. Tell the Lord how you feel about Him.
Thank Him for what this verse shows you about His nature.

_____
_____
_____
_____

Lord, what do you have to say to me through this verse?

_____
_____
_____
_____

What are some ways I can plant this truth deep in my heart?

_____
_____
_____
_____

What is going on in my life that I need to apply this verse to?

_____
_____
_____
_____

# Today's Verse

## Ponder & Pray

START WITH WORSHIP. TELL THE LORD HOW YOU FEEL ABOUT HIM.
THANK HIM FOR WHAT THIS VERSE SHOWS YOU ABOUT HIS NATURE.

_____

_____

_____

_____

LORD, WHAT DO YOU HAVE TO SAY TO ME THROUGH THIS VERSE?

_____

_____

_____

WHAT ARE SOME WAYS I CAN PLANT THIS TRUTH DEEP IN MY HEART?

_____

_____

_____

_____

WHAT IS GOING ON IN MY LIFE THAT I NEED TO APPLY THIS VERSE TO?

_____

_____

_____

_____

**Date**

## Today's Verse

### Ponder & Pray

Start with Worship. Tell the Lord how you feel about Him.
Thank Him for what this verse shows you about His nature.

_____

_____

_____

_____

Lord, what do you have to say to me through this verse?

_____

_____

_____

_____

What are some ways I can plant this truth deep in my heart?

_____

_____

_____

_____

What is going on in my life that I need to apply this verse to?

_____

_____

_____

_____

# Journal

Date

TAKE TIME TO SIT, REST, BREATHE...BE BEFORE THE LORD.
WHAT DOES HE HAVE TO SAY TO YOU?

# Dwell

"GREAT PEACE HAVE THOSE WHO LOVE YOUR LAW, AND NOTHING CAN MAKE THEM STUMBLE."

Psalm 119:165 Niv

# Today's Verse

**Date**

## Ponder & Pray

Start with Worship. Tell the Lord how you feel about Him. Thank Him for what this verse shows you about His nature.

_____

_____

_____

_____

Lord, what do you have to say to me through this verse?

_____

_____

_____

_____

What are some ways I can plant this truth deep in my heart?

_____

_____

_____

_____

What is going on in my life that I need to apply this verse to?

_____

_____

_____

_____

**Date**

## Today's Verse

### Ponder & Pray

Start with Worship. Tell the Lord how you feel about Him.
Thank Him for what this verse shows you about His nature.

_____
_____
_____
_____

Lord, what do you have to say to me through this verse?

_____
_____
_____
_____

What are some ways I can plant this truth deep in my heart?

_____
_____
_____
_____

What is going on in my life that I need to apply this verse to?

_____
_____
_____
_____

# Today's Verse

## Ponder & Pray

Start with Worship. Tell the Lord how you feel about Him.
Thank Him for what this verse shows you about His nature.

_____

_____

_____

_____

Lord, what do you have to say to me through this verse?

_____

_____

_____

_____

What are some ways I can plant this truth deep in my heart?

_____

_____

_____

_____

What is going on in my life that I need to apply this verse to?

_____

_____

_____

_____

**Date**

## Today's Verse

### Ponder & Pray

START WITH WORSHIP. TELL THE LORD HOW YOU FEEL ABOUT HIM.
THANK HIM FOR WHAT THIS VERSE SHOWS YOU ABOUT HIS NATURE.

_____
_____
_____
_____

LORD, WHAT DO YOU HAVE TO SAY TO ME THROUGH THIS VERSE?

_____
_____
_____
_____

WHAT ARE SOME WAYS I CAN PLANT THIS TRUTH DEEP IN MY HEART?

_____
_____
_____
_____

WHAT IS GOING ON IN MY LIFE THAT I NEED TO APPLY THIS VERSE TO?

_____
_____
_____
_____
_____

# Today's Verse

## Ponder & Pray

Start with Worship. Tell the Lord how you feel about Him.
Thank Him for what this verse shows you about His nature.

_____

_____

_____

_____

Lord, what do you have to say to me through this verse?

_____

_____

_____

_____

What are some ways I can plant this truth deep in my heart?

_____

_____

_____

_____

What is going on in my life that I need to apply this verse to?

_____

_____

_____

_____

**Date**

## Today's Verse

### Ponder & Pray

Start with Worship. Tell the Lord how you feel about Him.
Thank Him for what this verse shows you about His nature.

_____

_____

_____

_____

Lord, what do you have to say to me through this verse?

_____

_____

_____

_____

What are some ways I can plant this truth deep in my heart?

_____

_____

_____

_____

What is going on in my life that I need to apply this verse to?

_____

_____

_____

_____

# Journal

Date

Take time to sit, rest, breathe...be before the Lord.
What does he have to say to you?

# Dwell

"May my cry come before you, Lord; give me understanding according to your word."

Psalm 119:169 Niv

# Today's Verse

## Ponder & Pray

START WITH WORSHIP. TELL THE LORD HOW YOU FEEL ABOUT HIM.
THANK HIM FOR WHAT THIS VERSE SHOWS YOU ABOUT HIS NATURE.

_____

_____

_____

_____

LORD, WHAT DO YOU HAVE TO SAY TO ME THROUGH THIS VERSE?

_____

_____

_____

_____

WHAT ARE SOME WAYS I CAN PLANT THIS TRUTH DEEP IN MY HEART?

_____

_____

_____

_____

_____

WHAT IS GOING ON IN MY LIFE THAT I NEED TO APPLY THIS VERSE TO?

_____

_____

_____

_____

**Date**

## Today's Verse

### Ponder & Pray

Start with Worship. Tell the Lord how you feel about Him.
Thank Him for what this verse shows you about His nature.

_____

_____

_____

Lord, what do you have to say to me through this verse?

_____

_____

_____

What are some ways I can plant this truth deep in my heart?

_____

_____

_____

_____

What is going on in my life that I need to apply this verse to?

_____

_____

_____

_____

# Today's Verse

**Date**

## Ponder & Pray

Start with Worship. Tell the Lord how you feel about Him. Thank Him for what this verse shows you about His nature.

_____
_____
_____
_____

Lord, what do you have to say to me through this verse?

_____
_____
_____
_____

What are some ways I can plant this truth deep in my heart?

_____
_____
_____
_____

What is going on in my life that I need to apply this verse to?

_____
_____
_____
_____

**Date**

## Today's Verse

### Ponder & Pray

Start with Worship. Tell the Lord how you feel about Him.
Thank Him for what this verse shows you about His nature.

_____

_____

_____

_____

Lord, what do you have to say to me through this verse?

_____

_____

_____

_____

What are some ways I can plant this truth deep in my heart?

_____

_____

_____

_____

_____

What is going on in my life that I need to apply this verse to?

_____

_____

_____

_____

# Today's Verse

## Ponder & Pray

Start with Worship. Tell the Lord how you feel about Him. Thank Him for what this verse shows you about His nature.

_____

_____

_____

_____

Lord, what do you have to say to me through this verse?

_____

_____

_____

_____

What are some ways I can plant this truth deep in my heart?

_____

_____

_____

_____

What is going on in my life that I need to apply this verse to?

_____

_____

_____

_____

**Date**

## Today's Verse

## Ponder & Pray

Start with Worship. Tell the Lord how you feel about Him. Thank Him for what this verse shows you about His nature.

_____
_____
_____
_____

Lord, what do you have to say to me through this verse?

_____
_____
_____
_____

What are some ways I can plant this truth deep in my heart?

_____
_____
_____
_____
_____

What is going on in my life that I need to apply this verse to?

_____
_____
_____
_____

# Journal

TAKE TIME TO SIT, REST, BREATHE...BE BEFORE THE LORD.
WHAT DOES HE HAVE TO SAY TO YOU?

# Tree of Abiding

Use these tools to create and cultivate your own Tree of Abiding. Look back over all the verse you've written down. Which ones are foundational for you? Write the verse reference below. What specific words can you pull from those passages to serve as reminders of those truths? Write those words down next to the corresponding verse.

| Verses | Words |
|--------|-------|
|        |       |
|        |       |
|        |       |
|        |       |
|        |       |
|        |       |
|        |       |
|        |       |
|        |       |
|        |       |
|        |       |
|        |       |
|        |       |
|        |       |
|        |       |

Taking the words you gleaned from the verses you wrote, fill in those truths in the areas around the tree. For instance, if one of your verses was Psalm 34:8, you may glean the truth of God's goodness. Maybe for you a good place to put that would be in the roots of Identity. Or it maybe it also fits for you as a fruit of Influence.

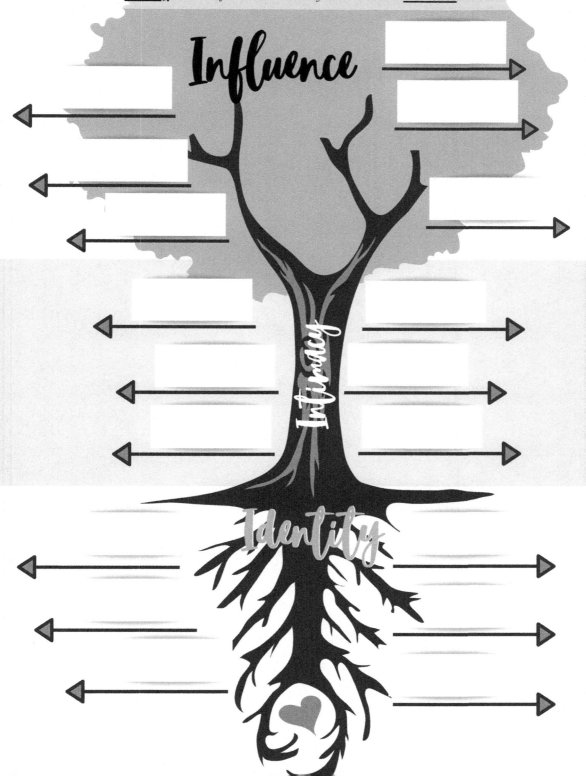

Date

# Journal

Take time to sit, rest, breathe...be before the Lord.
What does he have to say to you?

# Journal

TAKE TIME TO SIT, REST, BREATHE...BE BEFORE THE LORD.
WHAT DOES HE HAVE TO SAY TO YOU?

Date

Date

Journal

Take time to sit, rest, breathe...be before the Lord.
What does he have to say to you?

# Journal

Date

TAKE TIME TO SIT, REST, BREATHE...BE BEFORE THE LORD.
WHAT DOES HE HAVE TO SAY TO YOU?

**Date**

# Journal

TAKE TIME TO SIT, REST, BREATHE...BE BEFORE THE LORD.
WHAT DOES HE HAVE TO SAY TO YOU?

# Journal

TAKE TIME TO SIT, REST, BREATHE...BE BEFORE THE LORD.
WHAT DOES HE HAVE TO SAY TO YOU?

Date

# Journal

Take time to sit, rest, breathe...be before the Lord.
What does he have to say to you?

# Journal

Date

TAKE TIME TO SIT, REST, BREATHE...BE BEFORE THE LORD.
WHAT DOES HE HAVE TO SAY TO YOU?

# Other Books & Journals

## BOOKS

Milk & Honey in the Land of Fire & Ice
Becoming His:
Finding your place as a daughter of God

## JOURNALS & PLANNERS

Milk & Honey Women Study & Prayer Journal
The Cultivational Planner:
A Devotional planner for women

## About the Author/Designer

**Jenny Erlingsson** is wife to her amazing viking husband and mother to four cute and fierce mocha drops. After over twelve years of serving in pastoral ministry in Alabama, she and her family currently live in Iceland working in various areas of ministry. Jenny is passionate about empowering others, especially women through her writing and speaking. She is also the author of **Milk & Honey in the Land of Fire & Ice** and **Becoming His: Finding Your Place as a Daughter of God**

Made in United States
North Haven, CT
25 February 2022

16480377R00089